# Where Is the Bermuda Triangle?

# Where Is
# the Bermuda
# Triangle?

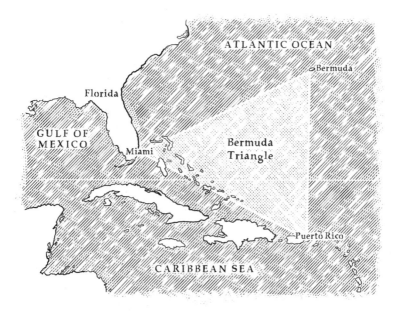

by Megan Stine

illustrated by Tim Foley

Penguin Workshop
An Imprint of Penguin Random House

PENGUIN WORKSHOP
Penguin Young Readers Group
An Imprint of Penguin Random House LLC

*Library of Congress Cataloging-in-Publication Data is available.*

ISBN 9781524786267 (paperback)          10 9 8 7 6 5 4 3 2 1
ISBN 9781524786281 (library binding)    10 9 8 7 6 5 4 3 2 1

# Contents

# Where Is the Bermuda Triangle?

On a beautiful sunny afternoon in 1945, five airplanes took off from a runway in Fort Lauderdale, Florida. The planes were US Navy bombers, but they weren't going to drop bombs. They were just out on a training run. The pilots were supposed to fly east, over the ocean, and then go north for a while before heading back home. The whole flight was supposed to last only two hours. The trip was called Flight 19.

But somehow, the pilots got lost and confused. They didn't know which way to go. The officer in charge had two compasses to show him directions. But *both* stopped working. He tried to contact the control tower for help, but his radio wasn't working well. Then another pilot flying nearby heard they were lost. He offered to come help, but the officer told him *not* to.

Before the day was over, all five planes had disappeared without a trace! The navy quickly sent another plane out to search for them—and it vanished, too!

How could this possibly happen? How could six planes and twenty-seven men vanish into thin air, never having sent an emergency signal? All the planes had life rafts on board. If the pilots had to land their planes in the ocean, wouldn't at least some of the pilots have survived?

For weeks, the navy searched a wide area of the sea. They never found a single thing—not even a piece of a broken plane floating in the water. Even now, more than seventy years later, the story makes people wonder whether there is something strange and unusual about the area the planes were flying through.

In fact, it is just one of the stories about the Bermuda Triangle—the name given to a triangular area in the ocean, off the coast of Florida, where dozens of ships and planes have disappeared.

Some stories say the Bermuda Triangle sucks ships into the sea. Others say that planes can enter the Bermuda Triangle but never escape. Over the years, ships have been found floating in the water—abandoned ships in perfect condition, with food still cooking on the stove, but no people on board! Huge oceangoing ships have been said to break in half in the treacherous seas. One year, at Christmastime, two men went out on a boat only a mile from the Florida coast. They wanted to gaze at the Christmas lights back on shore. They hit something in the water and called the Coast Guard for help. But when the Coast Guard arrived twenty minutes later, they had vanished. They were never seen or heard from again. To add to the spookiness of this story, their boat was called the *Witchcraft*.

This is the story of the mysterious area known as the Bermuda Triangle—who vanished, how they disappeared, and why.

# Air Traffic Control Towers

How do airplane pilots avoid running into each other in the sky? How do they know when it's their turn to take off or land at an airport? Who can help when a pilot gets lost during a flight?

The air traffic control tower is in charge. Every airport has a control tower with people inside who talk to pilots as they fly. The control tower tells each pilot how high above the ground they may fly that day—their altitude. The tower creates invisible "layers" of planes, like roads in the sky. This system keeps planes from crashing into each other by never flying in the same place or at the same altitude.

As a plane flies across the United States, it is always in radio contact with the nearest tower. But when Flight 19 got lost, their radio signals were poor. They couldn't always hear what the tower was saying.

# CHAPTER 1
## The Deadly Triangle

Where, exactly, is the dangerous area of water that—according to stories—has been the cause of so much tragedy? Draw three lines on a map connecting Bermuda, Puerto Rico, and Miami, Florida. The lines will make a triangle in the ocean. That's the location of the Bermuda Triangle.

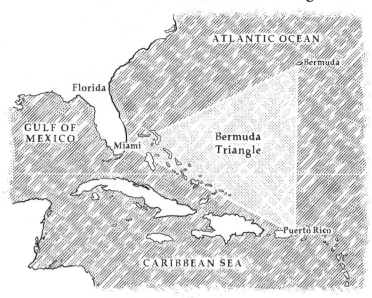

The ocean is unusually deep in the Bermuda Triangle. It's three miles deep in many places and over five miles deep in one spot. Hundreds of different species of small sea creatures live miles below the surface.

The first person ever known to sail near the Bermuda Triangle was Christopher Columbus. In 1492, he sailed west from Spain, hoping to find a new route to Asia. Instead, he wound up on an island off the coast of Florida—an island called San Salvador, that's now part of the Bahamas.

Christopher Columbus

But before he reached the Bahamas, Columbus experienced something very strange aboard his ship, the *Santa Maria*. He sailed into a vast area where the ocean was covered with a thick carpet

of weeds. The huge mat of weeds was rotating clockwise. It was like a slow-moving whirlpool. Creatures crawled all over the weeds—turtles, crabs, and eels. The air was strangely still.

Columbus thought he must be near land. Why else would there be so many plants growing on the

water? Plants didn't grow in the middle of the ocean—only near shore. But for days and days, he couldn't find land. The crew was alarmed. They wanted Columbus to turn back and sail home to Spain. Then something else happened to frighten the crew even more. Columbus's compass wasn't pointing toward the North Star, the way it usually did. Why wasn't it working? What was happening in this strange part of the ocean?

Columbus didn't know it, but he had sailed into what's now called the Sargasso Sea—a huge area of the Atlantic Ocean. It overlaps about half of the Bermuda Triangle.

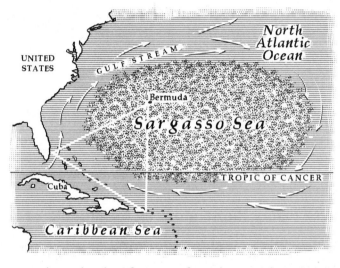

For hundreds of years after that, sailors passing through these waters told tales about the Sargasso Sea. They called it the "graveyard of ships" or the "sea of doom." According to the stories, ships could sail into it, but often they couldn't escape. Ghost ships supposedly sailed there forever, with skeletons on board as crews.

# The Sargasso Sea

The Sargasso Sea is a very strange place indeed. It is the only "sea within a sea" in the world—completely surrounded by the Atlantic Ocean. It's so different from the Atlantic Ocean that it has its own name. The Atlantic Ocean has strong currents, rolling waves, and high winds. The Sargasso Sea is usually calm, still, and covered with seaweed. Without wind, sailing ships can get stuck there, sometimes for days or weeks—or forever.

The sea is named for the sargassum seaweed that grows on the water.  Stretching more than two thousand miles long and around seven hundred miles wide, it is about half the size of the United States (not counting Alaska and Hawaii).

# The Horse Latitudes

One section of the Sargasso Sea is especially calm, with little wind or rain. It's in what are called the horse latitudes. (Latitudes are imaginary horizontal lines drawn around the earth on a globe or map.) The northern horse latitude runs straight across the northern part of the Sargasso Sea. Some stories say that hundreds of years ago, ships with horses on board became stranded there. The horses died from thirst, and the crew had to throw the dead animals overboard. Some sailors say that the ghosts of the horses still haunt those waters, even today.

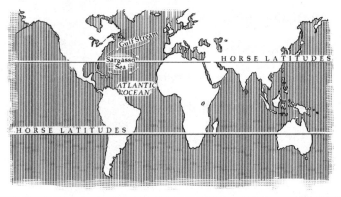

Columbus's crew was terrified when they heard about his compass pointing the "wrong" way. They were afraid that they'd never find land. But Columbus calmed them down. He said that maybe his compass wasn't supposed to point to the North Star. Maybe it was supposed to point to something else, although he didn't know what. Was he right? Years later, scientists learned more about how compasses work and found out that Columbus *was* right.

None of the stories about the Bermuda Triangle existed in Columbus's time. If they had, the crew would have been even more frightened on their voyage. Luckily for them, the wind picked up in the Sargasso Sea and less than a month later, Columbus found land.

Many other ships that sailed into the waters of the Bermuda Triangle were not nearly so fortunate.

## CHAPTER 2
## Lost at Sea

As the years went by, many ships were lost in the Bermuda Triangle.

In 1880, a huge ship called the *Atalanta* sailed from Bermuda toward England. On board were 290 men—officers and young cadets. The ship never reached England. None of the men were ever seen again.

The very next year, an even stranger thing happened. A ship called the *Ellen Austin* was sailing in the Atlantic, north of the Sargasso Sea.

All of a sudden someone on board spotted a derelict—a ghost ship. *Derelict* is the word for ships that are found drifting upright on the ocean with no one on board.

What had happened? Did it fall under the spell of some unknown force in that part of the ocean?

The captain of the *Ellen Austin* watched the ghost ship drifting for two days. He wanted to make sure it was really abandoned. He didn't want to walk into a trap set by pirates!

Finally, he decided it was safe. He sent some of his own men in a small rowboat to check out the drifting ship. When they boarded the ghost ship, they found the ship's log was missing and the name had been removed from the bow—the front of the ship. Other than that, though, it was in good condition—fully stocked with food.

So the captain ordered his men to sail the abandoned ship back to New York, staying close to the *Ellen Austin* along the way. In those days, if someone found an abandoned ship, there was reward money for bringing it back to the nearest port.

But the *Ellen Austin* and the ghost ship got separated by bad weather, fog, and strong winds. A few days later, the captain finally spotted the derelict again. But it was drifting crazily—and there was no one on board! His own men—the second crew—had vanished completely!

As time went by, more unexplained things occurred in or near the Bermuda Triangle.

In 1909, one of the world's greatest sailors was a man named Joshua Slocum. He was famous

Joshua Slocum

for being the first man to sail alone all the way around the world. On his journeys, he had survived huge storms, attacks by pirates, and worse. But he disappeared completely on a simple solo trip that led him straight through the Bermuda Triangle.

And then, in 1918, a huge US Navy ship called the *Cyclops* disappeared—without ever sending a single SOS. In those days, an SOS signal would be sent in Morse code whenever a ship or boat was in trouble on the seas.

The *Cyclops* had a radio. The crew could have

called for help. Why didn't they? There were 309 men on board. All vanished. It was the largest navy ship ever lost without a trace. It had been sailing from Barbados in the West Indies toward Chesapeake Bay. The route took it right through the heart of the Bermuda Triangle.

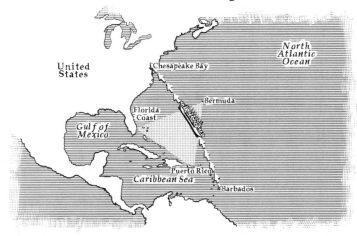

# Morse Code

Morse code uses a series of dots and dashes to stand for each letter of the alphabet. It was invented by Samuel Morse, who also invented the telegraph in 1844. With the telegraph, people were able to send messages through electric signals that traveled over wires using Morse code. Later, Morse code was used to send signals over radio waves.

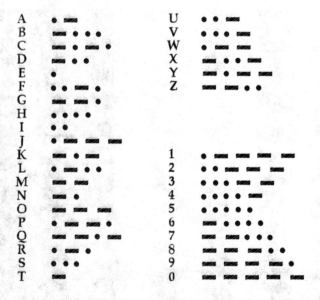

To send an SOS signal in Morse code, a radio operator would tap out a series of dots and dashes. The code for *S* is three dots (or three short signals). The code for *O* is three dashes (or three long signals). So the code for SOS is dot-dot-dot, dash-dash-dash, dot-dot-dot. The code can be sent as electronic sounds or even as short and long flashes of light with a flashlight or a mirror. Some people say that SOS stands for "Save Our Ship," but it was actually chosen as a distress signal because it was an easy message to send and understand, no matter what language operators were using.

SOS is not used very often anymore. Today, the word "mayday" is used as the international signal for distress—a sign that someone is in trouble. "Mayday" comes from a French phrase, *m'aider*, which means "help me." It is a crime to send a false SOS or mayday when nothing is wrong.

The *Cyclops* wasn't the last ship to run into strange troubles in those dangerous waters. Only a few years later, another ghost ship was found adrift. And this time, the story was filled with so many twists and turns, it could have been a spy movie.

## CHAPTER 3
## Another Ghost Ship

Three years after the *Cyclops* disappeared, another strange and mysterious event occurred in the Bermuda Triangle. A large five-masted ship called the *Carroll A. Deering* was spotted stuck on a sandbar off the coast of North Carolina.

No humans were on board, but a meal was still cooking on the stove. Most of the captain's and crew's things were missing—clothes, luggage, a heavy trunk. Two cats seemed to have the run of the place.

Had the captain and crew climbed into the lifeboats, trying to escape during a storm? If so, how could they have taken all those heavy bags with them?

Or had something weirder happened? All sorts of possibilities were put forth in the newspapers. Maybe there was a mutiny on board. A mutiny is when the crew of a ship rebels against the captain and takes over. Maybe the crew killed the captain and then rowed ashore in small boats. Other people thought pirates had come aboard and taken over.

There was very little, however, to back up most of these ideas. Then, in June 1921, the *New York Times* reported that a message had been found in a bottle on the shore in North Carolina. The message appeared to have been written by one of the crew members. It said the ship had been taken over—and the crew had been put in leg-irons!

The captain's wife hired a handwriting expert to look at the message. She wanted to know who had written it. For a while, she was convinced it had been written by Henry Bates, one of the crew members on her husband's ship. Later, though, the man who discovered the message in the bottle admitted that it was a hoax, or a trick.

Finally, the New York Police Department said maybe Russians were to blame. The police had heard stories about a Russian scheme. According to the stories, groups of Russians living in America would get themselves hired as sailors on a ship. Once at sea, they would mutiny. Then they'd sail the ship to a Russian port. Maybe Russians took over the ship and then had to abandon it during bad weather.

Years later, though, some people began to suspect another reason. They thought the *Carroll A. Deering* had been a victim of the Bermuda Triangle.

As time went by, the list of ships that had gone missing in the Bermuda Triangle kept piling up. In 1941, two more huge navy ships disappeared.

They were sister ships to the *Cyclops*. They had been sailing through the Triangle on a trip north to Portland, Maine.

A few years later, a ship called the *Rubicon* was found drifting off the coast of Florida—with only a dog on board. What had happened to the captain? Why were all his clothes still there?

# Is It a Boat or a Ship?

What's the difference between a boat and a ship? The US Naval Institute says, "You can put a boat on a ship, but you can't put a ship on a boat." What that means is that ships are big enough so that they can carry smaller boats on them—lifeboats, for instance. But boats are usually too small to carry other boats.

Some ships, however, are so big, they can carry another ship. The smaller ship riding on the gigantic one doesn't suddenly become a boat just because it's piggybacking.

Boat

Ship

In 1952, a writer named George X. Sand wrote an article about all the disappearances in the Atlantic Ocean. The article was printed in *Fate* magazine—a magazine that printed stories about ghosts and UFOs and other weird legends and mysteries. Sand described the triangular area of water where boats, ships, and planes seemed to disappear without a trace. But he didn't invent the name "Bermuda Triangle." The name was invented

by another writer, Vincent Gaddis, in 1964. He wrote a cover story about the mysterious Bermuda Triangle for a magazine called *Argosy*.

Ten years later, a writer named Charles Berlitz wrote a bestselling book that made the Bermuda Triangle a popular topic all over the world.

Some people thought the idea of a Bermuda Triangle was silly. They said it was easy to explain why boats would sink or vanish in the ocean. The ocean is huge. At times it is filled with enormous, powerful waves that roll and swirl. Of course huge waves can swallow up smaller boats or cause big ships to turn over.

But what about planes? How could anyone explain all the planes that disappeared over the very same triangular spot on the map?

# CHAPTER 4
## Lost in the Sky

After the five navy planes in Flight 19 vanished, more stories of disappearing airplanes began to mount up.

In 1948, a plane called the *Star Tiger* was headed toward Bermuda. The flight had started in London with thirty-one passengers and crew on board. The weather was beautiful in Bermuda that day, and the pilot called the tower to say the plane would arrive on time. But it didn't. After that radio call, the *Star Tiger* was never heard from again. The US Air Force immediately sent out a search team. They searched the ocean for five solid days. Not a single piece of the airplane was ever found.

The British investigated the disappearance, as

*Star Tiger*

the plane was British, and Bermuda is a British territory. They didn't turn up enough evidence to explain with certainty what had happened.

# Bermuda

Bermuda is a small group of beautiful islands in the Atlantic Ocean. It is famous for its pink sand beaches. It's located more than six hundred miles off the coast of North Carolina. The weather is always warm on the island, so men wear shorts to stay cool. Bermuda shorts are even considered fancy enough to be worn with a formal suit jacket and tie.

Bermuda was settled by the British in the early 1600s when some people from England were shipwrecked on their way to start a new colony in Virginia.

Bermuda never became part of the United States. It's still a British territory. Just like in England, people in Bermuda drive their cars on the left side of the road.

No one could ever figure out what happened to the *Star Tiger*. The plane had four engines—they couldn't have all died at once! The investigators said it was one of the most baffling problems they'd ever dealt with—and it would forever remain a mystery.

The very next year, the *Star Ariel* disappeared after taking off from Bermuda on a perfectly calm day. The *Star Ariel* was a sister to the *Star Tiger*—the same kind of plane. Somehow, without explanation and without ever calling for help, the sister plane vanished on the same route through the Triangle.

Meanwhile, another plane had gone missing near the coast of Florida in 1948. The passengers on the DC-3 were families on their way home to Miami from a Christmas vacation in Puerto Rico. It was a perfectly clear night—no storms to worry about at all. The pilot called the Miami control tower to say they were only fifty miles

away. They would be landing soon. Then the plane simply vanished forever.

In November 1956, a plane just like the rescue plane from Flight 19 exploded one night in midair after leaving from Bermuda. A huge ship in the

water below saw the explosion in the sky. And then, in January 1962, another Air Force plane vanished near the Triangle.

In August 1963, two large military jets took off together from an airfield in southern Florida. Something terrible happened to both planes, but neither pilot called for help. Why not? Broken pieces of the planes were found floating in different parts of the Atlantic Ocean—both in the Bermuda Triangle.

The Flying Boxcar plane

The next unexplained event happened in 1965. An Air Force plane called a C-119, or Flying Boxcar, took off from Florida, headed toward the Bahamas. The pilot called in to the tower when the plane was only about forty-five minutes away from its destination. Everything seemed fine—he reported no trouble. The weather was good, and the plane was expected to arrive on time. Instead, it vanished completely—no one knows why.

Then, in January 1967, three planes disappeared in the same week in the Bermuda Triangle—all in good weather.

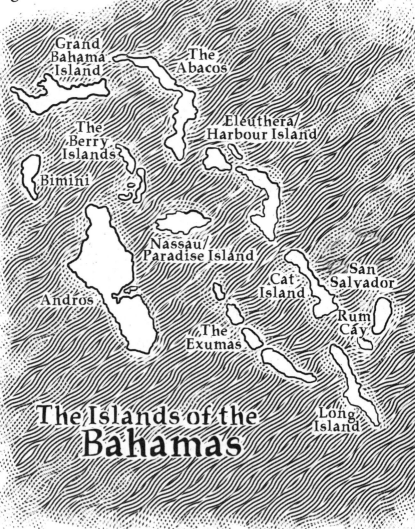

The Islands of the Bahamas

On Halloween in 1991, a Grumman Cougar jet flying near the Triangle disappeared from all radar screens in an instant. The plane was never seen again.

A number of years later, another plane vanished from the radar while flying toward Nassau, the capital of the Bahamas. Half an hour later, it popped back up on the radar screen. And then it disappeared forever.

And the mystery continues. By some counts, more than seventy-five planes have disappeared. What's happening? Is the power of the Bermuda Triangle getting stronger?

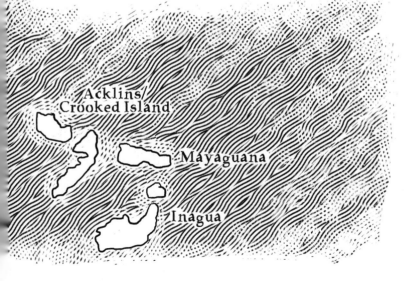

Acklins/
Crooked Island

Mayaguana

Inagua

# CHAPTER 5
## Strange Answers

What kind of strange, unnatural force could make ships and boats disappear in the Bermuda Triangle? Over the years, people have come up with a long list of possible explanations.

One idea is that there's something weird going on with the magnetic forces that surround earth near the Bermuda Triangle. There is some evidence that compasses do work strangely in the area. The leader on Flight 19 had trouble with his compasses. Other pilots have reported the same thing. Sometimes their compasses start spinning wildly and won't point to north at all. Even Christopher Columbus had trouble with his compass on his journey to the New World. Why? Does the Bermuda Triangle have a strange power over compasses?

To understand the answer, you need to know how compasses work. A compass is a tool that helps people know what direction they're going—north, east, south, or west. The compass has a magnetized needle or pointer inside. The needle is mounted on a pin so it can spin around. It is attracted to the magnetic forces that encircle the earth.

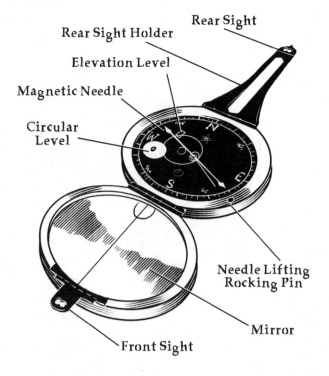

Rear Sight

Rear Sight Holder

Elevation Level

Magnetic Needle

Circular Level

Needle Lifting Rocking Pin

Mirror

Front Sight

Some people think a compass will always point to the North Star or the North Pole, called "true north." But that's not right. The needle always points to something called "magnetic north." Magnetic north isn't right at the North Pole. It's a spot near the North Pole where the magnetic forces come together.

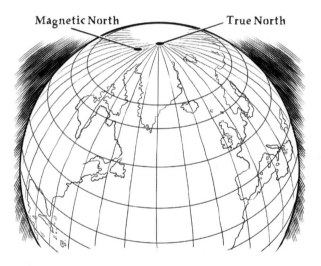

Magnetic North         True North

Magnetic north is always slowly moving around the globe. Why? Because the spinning of the earth is the force that creates the magnetic fields. And as the earth spins, the hot liquid core of the earth changes shape a little bit. It changes the magnetic fields. So magnetic north is always moving. Some days, it can be located fifty miles away from its usual spot. On average, though, it moves about six miles every year.

Today, sailors and pilots know that true north and magnetic north aren't always in the same place. Magnetic north is a few hundred miles away from the North Pole. So when pilots use a compass today, they always know they have to make a correction. They have to add or subtract from where the needle points. The amount of correction depends on where the pilot is on the globe.

When Columbus sailed to the New World, he didn't know that there was a difference between true north and magnetic north. But he guessed that his compass was pointing to something other than the North Star. He was right.

But was there some kind of strange magnetic

force near the Bermuda Triangle? No. In fact, the only thing that's unusual about the Bermuda Triangle is that it's lined up with one of the few places on earth where magnetic north and true north are often the same.

Sometimes compasses spin wildly in the Bermuda Triangle—but it's not some strange, unknown force making it happen. It can happen anywhere on earth. A compass needle will swing back and forth if the waves are choppy at sea.

Wild winds can make a compass needle dance around in an airplane. It doesn't mean there's anything strange going on. It just means compasses work best when they're held level and still.

In the 1970s, some people thought UFOs might be involved with the strange disappearances in the Bermuda Triangle. They said that each time a boat or plane disappeared in the area, the humans might have been kidnapped or captured by an alien spaceship! Where did this idea come from?

The UFO idea probably started when the Flying Boxcar disappeared in 1965. The Gemini IV spacecraft was circling the earth at the same time. Gemini IV was the first space mission in which American astronauts walked in space, outside the capsule. During the flight, astronaut James McDivitt reported that he saw a UFO just a day or so before the Flying Boxcar disappeared. He said the UFO was a white cylinder with "big arms" sticking out. He even took a picture of it.

James McDivitt

A few years later, a group of people who keep track of UFO stories put those two facts together. They came up with an idea about what happened to the Flying Boxcar. They claimed that aliens were there that day and might have snatched the plane right out of the air!

But James McDivitt reminded everyone that UFO stands for "unidentified flying object." It means anything flying that can't be identified—not just spaceships from another planet. There are hundreds—maybe thousands—of UFOs in space all the time. They are pieces of satellites that broke apart or pieces of rockets that broke off when a space shuttle was launched. These UFOs are sometimes called "space junk." James

Earth surrounded by space junk

McDivitt never claimed to have seen an alien spaceship over the Bermuda Triangle. He just said there was something in the sky he couldn't identify.

## Flight 19, UFOs, and *Close Encounters*

A famous movie director named Steven Spielberg had an idea about what might have happened to Flight 19. He used it in his movie *Close Encounters of the Third Kind*. It came out in  1977. The film starts when some scientists discover the five planes from Flight 19 in the desert in Mexico. The planes are in good shape and still working—but the pilots are gone. Soon, alien spacecraft are seen in the sky all over the world. At the end of the movie, a huge mother ship lands in the desert. When the spaceship doors open, people who had been captured by the aliens in the past are set free. The five pilots from Flight 19 are among the people who walk out of the mother ship. They haven't aged a day—even though it is thirty years later!

Other people have come up with an even stranger idea about the Bermuda Triangle. They think maybe planes and boats disappear because they are sucked into the ocean—and sink down into the lost world of Atlantis.

Atlantis is a mythical city that probably never existed. But it has been written about in stories and legends for thousands of years. In many of the stories, Atlantis was a very advanced, high-tech city. It was located on an island in the Atlantic Ocean. Later, according to the stories, the island sank deep into the sea. Some stories say the people of Atlantis had invented powerful flying vehicles and electricity. Others claim that some of the ancient buildings are still there, at the bottom of the ocean. They believe that powerful energy beams are still being sent out from the lost world of Atlantis! That's what has been snatching planes and ships.

There is no reason to believe that Atlantis ever existed—so it has nothing to do with the Bermuda Triangle. But the idea of a lost world is very popular. A beach hotel and resort in the Bahamas is named Atlantis. The hotel is built to look like an ancient city, with pyramids as water slides.

Atlantis is just one of many explanations for the mystery of the Bermuda Triangle. Another weird idea has to do with mercury in the ocean. Mercury is a metal—a metal that is liquid at normal temperatures on earth. Some of it seeps into the ocean naturally.

Liquid mercury

Some people said maybe mercury in the ocean was sending radio signals that made the planes crash. There is no scientific proof for this at all. It's just an idea that someone made up. Scientists don't think it's true.

Other nonsensical ideas about the Triangle included sea monsters and witchcraft. But maybe the wildest explanation for the Bermuda Triangle was that it's a "time warp." A time

warp is something made up by science-fiction writers. One famous children's book about time warps is called *A Wrinkle in Time.* In a time warp, people and things can travel through time, or time can speed up and slow down.

If a plane entered a time warp, it would disappear from the normal world. Supposedly it could fly to somewhere else. We don't have any reason to believe that time warps exist.

With so many weird ideas floating around, how could anyone know what's true? One man decided to investigate the Bermuda Triangle—to find out what really happened when all those ships and planes disappeared.

# The Devil's Sea

Is there another place in the world like the Bermuda Triangle—where boats and planes disappear mysteriously?

Some people point to a spot off the east coast of Japan as being a twin to the Bermuda Triangle. They call it the Devil's Sea. It's a twin because it's at the same distance from the equator as the Bermuda Triangle—but on the opposite side of the globe.

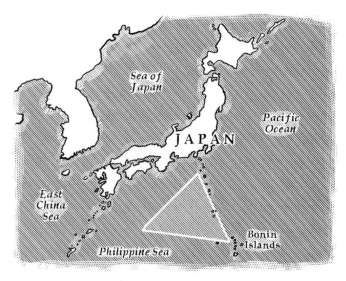

In the 1950s, several ships disappeared in the Devil's Sea. The Japanese government declared the spot dangerous—and told sailors to stay away. Why?

It turned out that there was an active underwater volcano at that spot in the ocean at the time. When the volcano erupted, it sank at least one huge ship. Other ships may have gone down for the same reason. While the volcano was active, it *was* a dangerous spot, but there was nothing spooky or supernatural going on.

# CHAPTER 6
## The Librarian Detective

In the early 1970s, a librarian named Larry Kusche decided to solve the mystery of the Bermuda Triangle. His interest was sparked after people kept calling or visiting the library, wanting to learn about the Triangle. Larry decided to do some research himself. Was something mysterious going on?

Larry Kusche

First, he made a list of every book and article written on the subject. Then he got in touch with the US Coast Guard, the US Air Force, and an insurance company

called Lloyd's of London.
Lloyd's insured ships,
so it was often involved
whenever a ship was lost
at sea. Larry also read
dozens of newspaper
reports. He even went
back to newspapers
printed in 1840!

Lloyd's of London

Little by little, he began to find facts that explained away the mysteries in Bermuda Triangle disappearances.

For one thing, it turned out that in many cases, the facts had not been reported correctly. Sometimes newspapers would say that a ship sank in good weather—but in truth, there had been a storm offshore. (Larry knew this because he would check out local weather reports from the day of a disappearance.) Sometimes boats were said to be lost in the Bermuda Triangle when they really sank a thousand miles away.

One by one, the truth about some of the mysteries came out.

Flight 19 had seemed so mysterious at first. How could five planes disappear all at once? But the navy had investigated and found a different story. They talked to all the people who had spoken to the pilots that day. Most of them were airport tower radio operators. But one was a pilot named Lieutenant Robert Cox.

Cox explained that he was flying near southern Florida that day when he heard some

Robert Cox

radio messages coming through. The voice said, "I don't know where we are. We must have got lost after that last turn." It was the voice of the Flight 19 leader, Lieutenant Charles Taylor. With neither of his compasses working, Taylor wasn't sure which way to go. Worse, he wasn't sure where he was. He thought he was flying over some islands south of Florida, called the Florida Keys. But Taylor was new to the Florida area. He wasn't as familiar with those islands—or the Bahamas—as someone else might have been.

Charles Taylor

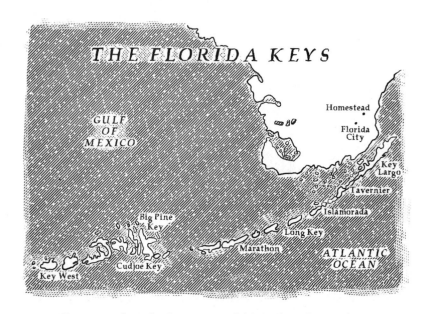

Cox tried to help. He told Taylor "put the sun on your port wing." That meant for Taylor to make sure the sun was on his left side. Since it was afternoon, the sun was in the west. With the sun on his left, Taylor would be flying north, up the coast of Florida. He should find Fort Lauderdale easily. Cox also offered to fly south to meet Taylor and the other planes.

"I know where I am now," Taylor said. "Don't come after me."

But did he know? Or was he still confused? For the rest of the afternoon, the radio messages from Taylor and the other pilots faded in and out. Sometimes the airport towers could hear Taylor.

Sometimes not. They asked him to switch to a different radio channel—one that would come in better. But Taylor refused. He was afraid that if he changed to another channel, he would lose contact with the young pilots in the other planes.

Over the next few hours, a lot of weak radio messages were heard. Some of the pilots had working compasses. They thought they should fly west to reach land. But they weren't in charge—they were being trained. Lieutenant Taylor was giving the orders, and he kept changing his mind. He told them to fly east, then west, then east again.

"If we would just fly west we would get home," two different pilots said.

They had been flying a long time—too long. They were running out of gas. If they didn't find land soon, they'd have to "ditch." That meant land in the water.

Finally, the lieutenant made a terrible decision. He told the other pilots, "When the first man gets down to ten gallons of gas, we will all land in the water together. Does everyone understand that?"

The planes remained lost for more than

four hours. As evening fell, the weather turned windy—and in the end, they ran out of gas.

Flying over the ocean, they simply never spotted land. What happened to them wasn't a mystery—it was a tragedy. It wasn't some strange, powerful force in the Bermuda Triangle that sucked them into the ocean. It was a combination of unlucky events—the broken compasses, the bad radio signals, and the decisions made by Lieutenant Taylor.

What about the rescue plane that went out to find them? How could it vanish so quickly? The answer was pretty simple. An explosion was seen in the sky about twenty minutes after the rescue plane took off. The rescue plane was a Martin Mariner. Some people called them "flying gas tanks" because they carried a large amount of fuel and were often filled with gas fumes. Fires could start easily. Another Martin Mariner exploded the same way, in 1956. Most

likely, both Mariners blew up when a spark of some kind lit the gas fumes.

But could all the disappearances in the Bermuda Triangle be explained so easily?

# CHAPTER 7
## Mysteries Solved

When Larry Kusche did more research, he found out that many more of the Bermuda Triangle mysteries were not so hard to explain. The disappearance of the *Atalanta*—the British ship with hundreds of young cadets on board—was no mystery at all.

By reading the London *Times* from 1880, Larry Kusche was able to find out the truth. There had

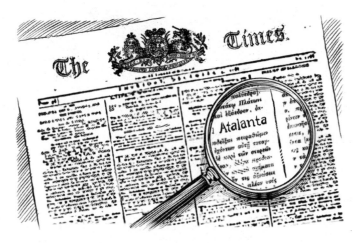

been heavy, violent storms in the Atlantic Ocean that lasted for almost a month! Other ships were lost at sea during the same time. Bad weather and rough seas are not "magical forces" that suck ships into the Bermuda Triangle. They are a constant danger at sea. Storms are often the cause of ships and planes going down all over the world.

Bad weather might also have been to blame for the loss of the *Cyclops.* Larry Kusche found a weather report that other people had overlooked. It said there was a huge storm near Norfolk, Virginia, around the same time that the *Cyclops* was lost. The winds blew at sixty miles per hour.

George W. Worley, captain of the *Cyclops*

Or there could have been another reason for

the disappearance of the *Cyclops*. It was a navy ship, and it vanished during World War I. America was at war with Germany. And guess what? The captain of the *Cyclops* was German! Some people thought the captain might have turned the ship over to the Germans to help them in the war.

Twenty-one years later, another war broke

out again with Germany. It was called World War II. And again, two more navy ships just like the *Cyclops* disappeared in the Bermuda Triangle in 1941. Was it a mystery force at work? No. Both ships were probably sunk by the Germans, who were trying to destroy enemy ships in the Atlantic.

And what about Joshua Slocum? The world's best sailor, who had sailed around the world? There are lots of guesses about what happened to him. There might have been an accident. For example, his boat might have been destroyed by a huge steamship in the night. Or he might

have had a heart attack and died. With no one to control the sails, the boat could have capsized (tipped over) and sunk. Or he might have been lost in a terrible storm. Even great sailors make costly mistakes. And furthermore, no one knows for sure *where* his ship went down.

Slocum set sail from Martha's Vineyard, which is off the coast of Massachusetts. Sure, he was heading toward the Bermuda Triangle. But maybe his boat sank while he was still many miles away. Blaming his disappearance on the Bermuda Triangle doesn't make sense when there were so many other possibilities.

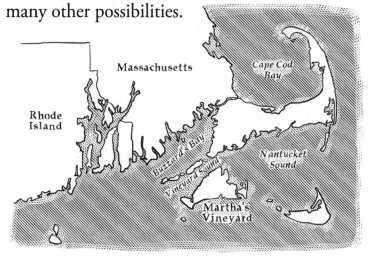

Another mystery that's easy to solve is the case of the *Rubicon*—the ship that was found drifting with only a dog on board. Was the captain snatched away by aliens from outer space? No. As a newspaper report explained, a hurricane came up—and the rope that held the *Rubicon* to the dock was broken. Strong winds probably tore the ship loose and set it drifting. The captain and crew had likely gone ashore before the hurricane hit.

Bad weather is common in the Bermuda Triangle. Not only can storms come up suddenly, but the Atlantic Ocean also has its own hurricane season in the summer and fall. Many of these hurricanes never reach land.

# Hurricanes

A hurricane is a huge, strong storm that rotates or spins in a spiral shape. To be called a hurricane, the winds must be at least seventy-four miles per hour. Hurricanes form over the ocean, and then sometimes move inland. Strong winds and high waves usually follow. In other parts of the world, the same kind of storm has a different name. In Japan, they are called typhoons. In the South Pacific, they're cyclones.

Waterspouts and methane gas are two more forces of nature that can sink ships and boats. Waterspouts are huge columns of water. They shoot up from the ocean like a tornado of spinning water that's being sucked into a cloud. Huge methane gas bubbles can also shoot up from the bottom of the sea. One theory goes that the bubbles are so big, they can sink boats or ships, although there's no proof that this has ever happened.

Waterspout

Airplanes can get into trouble in bad weather, too. But more often, an airplane crashes for different reasons. The *Star Tiger*, which vanished in 1948, had a number of problems. There were things wrong with the plane's mechanical parts—things that hadn't been fixed. Also, the plane was filled with so much fuel, it was actually "overweight"—a little too heavy. And the plane was flying at a very low altitude—only about two thousand feet above the earth. (Normally, a plane that size would fly as high as twenty thousand feet.) It's harder for a pilot to control a plane

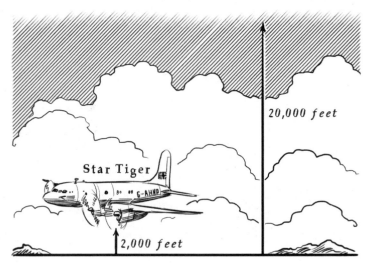

that's flying so low. If a mistake is made, there isn't as much room to correct the problem before crashing.

No one knows for sure what happened to the *Star Tiger*. But after its sister plane, the *Star Ariel*, disappeared the next year, the British airline company stopped using those planes for passenger flights. The airline seemed to believe that kind of plane was no longer safe, no matter where it flew.

How about the disappearance of the DC-3 plane bringing families home from Christmas vacation? Yes, the weather was clear. But the plane had weak batteries, so the radio signals were not strong. The pilot lost touch with the control tower. Winds might have blown the pilot off course. And the pilot and copilot had been flying for twenty hours that day. They could have been tired. These are more likely explanations for why the plane went down—not a spooky force in the Bermuda Triangle.

The two military planes that disappeared in 1963 are not a mystery at all. When the air force investigated, they found proof that the two planes had collided—they had run into each other in midair.

And what about the Flying Boxcar that

disappeared in 1965? Did a UFO grab that plane out of the sky? Not likely. The more logical explanation is that one of the plane's two engines died. With only one engine, the pilot would have had a very hard time keeping the plane in the air.

One thing, however, remains true about flying through the Bermuda Triangle. The skies can be very hazy and strange at times. One pilot named George Smith reported his experiences. George explained how easy it is to get confused. He said that sometimes the ocean and the sky blended together so much, he didn't know which was which. Sometimes he didn't know whether his plane was upside down or right side up! He couldn't trust his eyeballs. When that happens, George said, a pilot can be heading toward the water in a spiral and not even realize it. Pilots can crash into the ocean without ever sending out an SOS. The same thing can happen at night, too. Sometimes, if it's hazy, the stars look like the lights on the ground. Pilots don't know which way is up.

But not every mystery in the Bermuda Triangle can be explained so easily. Some mysteries are still unsolved—even today.

# CHAPTER 8
# Unsolved!

We will probably never find out what happened to ghost ships such as the *Carroll A. Deering*. The crew might have mutinied. Or the captain might have been involved in some sneaky plot. Or maybe it simply ran into bad weather. Maybe everyone climbed into a lifeboat, and then they were lost at sea. It's hard to know for sure, especially after so many years.

The *Ellen Austin* and the derelict ship that it found remains a double mystery. It seemed almost too spooky to be true.

Was it real? Or was it just a ghost story?

No one knows for sure. But Larry Kusche couldn't find a single newspaper report from the 1880s about the *Ellen Austin* encountering an unnamed mystery ship—and that was a time when newspapers almost always reported about missing ships.

The first person to write about the *Ellen Austin* was Rupert Gould. He was a British naval officer who later became a writer and a radio personality. He was interested in weird, unexplained events such as UFOs and the Loch Ness Monster. It's hard to know for sure whether the *Ellen Austin* story ever happened—or whether someone made the whole thing up.

Hoax photo of the Loch Ness Monster

# *Mary Celeste*:
## The Most Famous Ghost Ship

In 1872, a ship named the *Mary Celeste* sailed out of New York harbor. The captain, his wife, and his two-year-old daughter were on board along with a crew of seven men. The ship was carrying seventeen hundred barrels of alcohol to Italy.

But the *Mary Celeste* never reached Europe. Instead, it was found drifting in the ocean a month later, off the coast of Portugal. The sails were set and

Captain Briggs and his family

there was plenty of food on board. One report even said that dinner was on the table with coffee still in the cups. Toys were scattered on the captain's bed, as if his daughter had just been playing there. There were no signs of violence anywhere on the ship. The captain,  his family, and the crew were never seen again.

What happened? Many stories were told over the years, but no one ever found out the truth. Some people thought the crew drank the alcohol and then murdered the captain. Others thought the captain was in on a plot. Maybe he was going to claim the ship had sunk and then collect the insurance money. Or maybe the captain, his family, and the crew simply abandoned their ship when they thought it was going to sink. Then their lifeboat sank, but the *Mary Celeste* didn't.

Although the *Mary Celeste* didn't sail through the Bermuda Triangle, it's still one of the greatest sea mysteries of all time.

For anyone who wants to believe that the Bermuda Triangle has some magical force, those unsolved mysteries count as "proof" that something weird is going on. But scientists think differently. Scientists would say there are many unanswered questions in the world. Sometimes we just don't have enough information to answer them yet—or haven't taken the time to find out the truth.

The US Coast Guard does not believe the

Bermuda Triangle has magic power, either. They point out that it's a high-traffic area. Compared to the number of boats, ships, and planes passing through the Triangle, the number that "mysteriously" disappear is extremely small. Just as many boats vanish in other parts of the world where the boating traffic is heavy, according to the US Coast Guard. And since the weather is so unpredictable in the Bermuda Triangle, it's no surprise that sailors sometimes find themselves in trouble on the seas.

Maybe the simple truth is this: The Bermuda Triangle *is* a special, unusual place. With the crystal-clear blue waters of the Bahamas, it is a place many people want to visit. The tropical islands, coral reefs, and beautiful beaches attract people to the area all year round. Boats and planes full of tourists are drawn to the Bahamas, Puerto Rico, and Bermuda itself—a charming island with a fancy, old-fashioned feel.

Maybe the Bermuda Triangle isn't sucking ships and planes to the bottom of the ocean— it's simply pulling people toward one of the most magical, beautiful places in the world.

# Timeline of the Bermuda Triangle

1492 — Columbus has compass problems in the Sargasso Sea

1880 — British ship *Atalanta* leaves Bermuda and vanishes

1881 — Ship *Ellen Austin* supposedly spots a ghost ship and tries to save it; the second crew disappears

1909 — World's "best" sailor, Joshua Slocum, is lost at sea, possibly in the Bermuda Triangle

1918 — Navy ship *Cyclops* disappears without sending an SOS

1921 — Ghost ship *Carroll A. Deering* is found abandoned off North Carolina

1945 — Five US Navy planes disappear off the coast of Florida, as does a rescue plane sent to find them

1948 — Airliner *Star Tiger* disappears on its way to Bermuda

— DC-3 plane vanishes at Christmastime with passengers aboard

1964 — The term "Bermuda Triangle" is coined by a writer

1965 — Flying Boxcar vanishes only forty-five minutes away from the Bahamas

1967 — Three planes disappear in one week over the Triangle

1975 — Librarian Larry David Kusche publishes a book solving the mystery of the Triangle

1977 — The movie *Close Encounters of the Third Kind* depicts pilots from Flight 19

1991 — Cougar jet disappears on Halloween

# Timeline of the World

|  |  |
|------|-------|
| 1492 | Christopher Columbus sails to the "New World" |
| 1844 | Samuel Morse invents the telegraph and Morse code |
| 1869 | First transcontinental railroad completed in the United States |
| 1879 | Thomas A. Edison invents the practical electric lightbulb |
| 1881 | President James A. Garfield is shot and killed |
| 1908 | Ford introduces the Model T car |
| 1912 | The *Titanic* hits an iceberg and sinks |
| 1914 | World War I begins in Europe |
| 1917 | The United States enters World War I |
| 1931 | Empire State Building is completed |
| 1945 | World War II ends when United States drops two atomic bombs on Japan |
| 1948 | Israel is founded as a country |
| 1955 | Disneyland opens in Anaheim, California |
| 1957 | Soviet Union launches Sputnik 1, the first spacecraft |
| 1963 | Martin Luther King Jr. gives his "I Have a Dream" speech in Washington, DC |
| 1967 | First heart transplant surgery is performed |
| 1976 | Apple Computer is founded by Steve Jobs and Steve Wozniak |
| 1983 | Sally Ride becomes the first American woman in space |
| 1991 | The Internet becomes available to the public |

# Bibliography

**\*Books for young readers**

\* Bingham, Jane. *The Bermuda Triangle*. Chicago: Heinemann
Raintree, 2013.

\* Donkin, Andrew. *Bermuda Triangle*. New York: DK Publishing,
2000.

Kusche, Larry David. *The Bermuda Triangle Mystery—Solved*.
Amherst, NY: Prometheus Books, 1986.

\* Walker, Kathryn. *Mysteries of the Bermuda Triangle*. New York:
Crabtree Publishing, 2009.